A SECOND SUSSEX QUIZ BOOK

Winkling out the where, what and why
of the whacky, weird and wonderful

David Arscott

Illustrated by Tizzie Knowles

S.B. Publications

Books by the same author include:

Living Sussex
The Sussex Story
Sussex - the County in Colour
Curiosities of East Sussex
Curiosities of West Sussex
The Upstart Gardener
A Sussex Quiz Book

Video narration:

Discovering Brighton
Discovering West Sussex

First published in 1995 by S.B. Publications
c/o Grove Road, Seaford East Sussex BN25 1TP

ISBN 1 85770 086 4

Typeset and printed by Island Press Ltd.,
3 Cradle Hill Industrial Estate, Seaford, East Sussex BN25 3JE.
Telephone: (01323) 490222

CONTENTS

	Page
Introduction	4
1. Sussex by the Sea	5
2. Something in Common	6
3. Miscellaneous	7
4. A Woman's World	8
5. Churches	9
6. On the Road	10
7. Drink and be Merry	11
8. Gone but not Forgotten	12
9. Villages	13
10. Writers	14
11. The Year in Question	15
12. Bricks and Mortar	16
13. This Sporting Life	17
14. Miscellaneous	18
15. The Way We Were	19
16. Towns	20
17. Wildlife	21
18. Death Notices	22
19. Parks and Gardens	23
20. Sussex Book of Records	24
21. Dialect	25
22. Come Rain, Come Shine	26
23. Religious Types	27
24. Industrial History	28
25. Rivers	29
26. Miscellaneous	30
27. Schools	31
28. Follies	32
Countryside picture quiz	33-40
Towns picture quiz	41-48
Answers	49-64

Front cover photograph: Where is this pub sign, and why does it have a cat on it?

Back cover: What is the emblem on the Laughton village sign?

(Answers on p. 64)

INTRODUCTION

'Will you not tell us how a pig is cured,' asks a character in Belloc's *The Four Men,* 'for I long to learn one useful thing in my life.'

Ah, what a chord that strikes in the hearts of the bookish among us, ever conscious that one kind of knowledge all too often drives out another! Useless facts are far easier to come by than practical experience, and this book is packed with them. While a thorough reading of it will disclose, among much else, the materials used in trug making, the site of the last conical brick-built kiln in the county and the contents of a Sussex pond pudding, you will be no better placed to fashion baskets, make bricks or cook stodgy desserts than you were at the outset. Any dead pigs you may be harbouring must, alas, remain uncured.

The object of the exercise, then, is pure entertainment. I have followed the rules laid out in the first volume ('an impetus in favour of both fairness and fun,' if I may quote myself), and have again posed the questions in no particular order of difficulty: this means that they can be chosen at random by fireside or saloon bar competitors.

If asking questions is, by and large, far easier than answering them, the compiler of a second quiz book nevertheless has to set himself the minor chore of ensuring that he avoids repeating himself. Readers maddened by the brain-teasers which follow may take at least a little comfort in imagining their persecutor's painstaking attempts to achieve that goal. Although no question appears here exactly as before, however, an occasional sideways approach to the original material seems entirely in order, and a few characters and **incidents** do therefore reemerge in cunning disguise.

A final tip. Should the relentlessness of these three hundred questions fray the nerves, take Belloc's advice regarding the curing of his pig: 'When, therefore, you have so rubbed in a rubbard manner until your rubment is aglow with the rubbing, why then desist; hang up your half pig on a hook from a beam, and wash your hands and have done for that day.'

David Arscott

1. SUSSEX BY THE SEA

*Since 'the Queen of the Dippers',
Martha Gunn, has attracted more
than her fair share of the limelight,
our opening round is dedicated to her
male counterpart on the beaches of
Regency Brighton, John 'Smoaker'
Miles - a man apparently so confident
of his friendship with the Prince
Regent that he once pulled back his
royal client by the ear when he
strayed too far from the shore.*

1. Why do some of the grander houses along Hove seafront have three taps over the bath?

2. Why do several bungalows along West Front Road at Pagham have a series of small windows set into their walls?

3. What happened to the White Rock after which the Hastings theatre is named?

4. An attempted murder in Graham Greene's novel *Brighton Rock* takes place in an unfinished settlement whose dereliction suggests 'the last effort of despairing pioneers to break new country. The country had broken them.' Where was this?

5. The arrival on holiday of George III's daughter Amelia was important in promoting a Sussex seaside town as a fashionable watering-place. Which one?

6. What's unusual about the beach at the foot of Fairlight Glen?

7. Many of the country's pioneer film-makers lived in a small coastal community not far from Brighton. Which was it?

8. Off which town was *HMS Brazen* wrecked in 1800 with the loss of 105 lives?

9. What's odd about the road called Seaside in Eastbourne?

10. Built in 1866, it was 1,150ft long before part of it was demolished. What is it?

2. SOMETHING IN COMMON

The youngest Sussex highwayman on record shares a name with the man whose sea-water cure helped launch Brighton as a fashionable resort. Thirteen-year-old Richard Russell was charged at the assizes in 1796 with robbing the Hurst Green Mail and spent six months in prison. You may care to devise your own penalty for failure to perform well in this round.

What have, or had, the following in common:

1. The villages of Falmer, Friston, Lindfield and Wivelsfield Green?

2. Bateman's at Burwash, Gravetye Manor and Rowfant House?

3. Patcham, Truleigh Hill and Warningcamp, near Arundel?

4. Chailey Heritage School, Newhaven Downs Hospital and Wisborough Green village hall?

5. Herstmonceux Castle, Michelham Priory and the remains of Laughton Place?

6. Halnaker, Punnetts Town and Hog Hill, Icklesham?

7. Balcombe, Weir Wood and Darwell, near Robertsbridge?

8. John Street, Brighton and St John Street, Lewes?

9. *Alice in Wonderland* author Lewis Carroll and Karl Marx's collaborator Friedrich Engels?

10. Alciston, Patcham, Sullington and Wilmington?

3. MISCELLANEOUS

A round which ranges 'skitterwaisen', as a Sussex dialect speaker might have said, through your knowledge of art and architecture, industrial history, crime, shipwrecks and a little more besides.

1. The East Cliff lift at Hastings is electrically powered nowadays, but what originally moved it?

2. There are numerous earthen humps on Ashdown Forest which Ordnance Survey maps show as 'pillow mounds'. What are they?

3. The first Sussex skirmish of the Civil War took place on open ground at a spot now heavily populated. Where?

4. Sussex had a thriving Wealden iron industry in the sixteenth century. Which other industry was based in the Kirdford area at the same time?

5. The architect Benjamin Latrobe built Hammerwood Park, near Forest Row. Which famous American building was he responsible for?

6. Which notorious crime did Patrick Magee commit in Brighton?

7. Which two woods are used in the manufacture of Sussex trug baskets?

8. What was the American art connoisseur Edward Perry Warren keen to give to Lewes, where he lived, only to have the offer rejected?

9. Outside which public building will you find the Indian Jaipur Gate?

10. The Greek cargo ship *Athina B* ran aground on the beach at Brighton in January, 1979. What was she carrying?

4. A WOMAN'S WORLD

*'I am told on good authority
that when a Sussex damsel
says 'Oh! do adone' she
means you to go on; but when
she says 'Adone-do' you must
leave off immediately.'*
(The Rev W.D.Parish glossing the
word 'adone' in his Dictionary
of the Sussex Dialect)

1. What unusual kind of school did the Hon Frances Wolseley run at Glynde in the early twentieth century?

2. Ote Hall Chapel at Wivelsfield was founded by an 18th century evangelical Methodist who was responsible for many others throughout the country. Who was she?

3. Which dancer married, and later divorced, the eccentric West Dean millionaire Edward James?

4. Debi Raggio launched a new enterprise in Brighton during the 1990s with women's saftey in mind. What was it?

5. An old drovers' road from Patcham to Stanmer Park became popular with horsewomen during the late 19th century, which accounts for its modern name. What is it?

6. Which famous Yorkshire author refused an offer of marriage from the curate of Earnley, near Chichester?

7. Where in Sussex, in 1919, was England's first Women's Institute market opened?

8. Which well-loved singer founded an orphanage in Sussex?

9. The Knots of May is for women only. What do they do?

10. What did Dame Grace Kimmins found in 1903?

5. CHURCHES

'Dulcis sisto melis campana vocor Gabrielis'
('I am the honey-voiced bell called Gabriel').

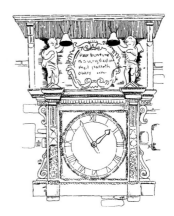

- *inscription on a church bell at Catsfield*

1. Where did the Quakers build their first meeting house in Sussex?

2. What's unusual about the approach to the church at Coombes, near Lancing?

3. What is laid down in Arundel Cathedral at the Feast of Corpus Christi?

4. Seven monks' faces adorn a 14th century sculpture in Linchmere church, near the Surrey border. What do they represent?

5. A musical instrument in Brightling church was donated by the eccentric squire 'Mad Jack' Fuller. What is it?

6. George IV's 'unofficial' wife, Maria Fitzherbert, was buried in the first Roman Catholic church to be built in the south of England since the Reformation. Which was it?

7. Why does Berwick church, near Lewes, have plain windows rather than stained glass?

8. Which church clock carries a quotation from the Apocrypha?

9. What name is commonly given to the low, pyramidal roofs which are a feature of Sussex country churches?

10. What, in 1993, did Gary Bevans finish painting on the ceiling of the English Martyrs Church at Worthing?

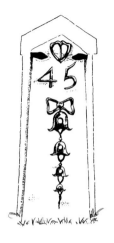

6. ON THE ROAD

'I write to you from this place as soon as I arrive, to tell you I have come off without hurt, both in my going and return through the Sussex ways, which are bad and ruinous beyond imagination. I vow 'tis a melancholy consideration that mankind will inhabit such a heap of dirt for a poor livelihood.'

(Lord Chancellor Cowper in a letter to his wife, 1690)

1. Where will you find the carving of a huge fossil shell at the entrance to a road tunnel?

2. Travelling west from Bolney on the A272, what's the first village you come to?

3. Name the odd one out among these four Sussex roads: the A27, the A259, the A24 and the A272.

4. Where is the first railway crossing on the A27 east of Lewes?

5. Sutton, Bignor, West Burton.... What's the next village, travelling west to east?

6. What do the A22; the A26 between Uckfield and Lewes; and the A268 from Kent down to Rye have in common?

7. The road from Albourne to Sayers Common, north of Brighton, used to be part of the A23 until the villages were bypassed. What is the road's number now?

8. Do you pass through the Pylons when driving *into* Brighton or *out of* the town?

9. Which roads through Sussex form part of the Folkestone-Honiton trunk route?

10. London 53 miles; Arundel 18 miles; Bognor Regis 18 miles; Chichester 12 miles. Where am I?

7. DRINK AND BE MERRY

*'I went down to Jones's,
where we drank one bowl of
punch and two mugs
of bumboo; and I came home
again in liquor.'*

*(Another bad night for the East
Hoathly diarist Thomas Turner)*

1. Which musician's face appeared on the sign of the Queen's Head at Bolney during the early 1990s?

2. What's the name of the pub at Ditchling crossroads?

3. The pub at Alciston was once a family home. What is its name?

4. Which service, unusual for a pub, is offered by the Black Horse at Binsted, near Arundel.

5. Which pub name is common to Ardingly, Brighton, Henfield and Lewes?

6. What was the name of the Piltdown Man pub at Piltdown before Charles Dawson's bogus archaeological discovery?

7. The Red Lion at Willingdon features in a famous twentieth century novel. Which one?

8. Where will you find a pub called the Bent Arms?

9. Nicholas Tettersell, who sailed the future Charles II to safety in France, later owned what is now Brighton's oldest inn. Which one?

10. Which pub name is common to Barcombe Cross, Poynings and Wineham?

8. GONE BUT NOT FORGOTTEN

*The World is a round thing
And full of crooked streets.
Death is a market place
Where all Men meets.
If Life was a thing
That money could buy
The Rich would live
And the Poor would dye.*

(Gravestone to Alice Woolldridge,
buried at Poling in 1740)

1. Complete the rhyme on the tombstone of John Parson, who died of pulmonary tuberculosis in 1633 and was buried at West Tarring:

   *Youth was his Age, Virginity his State,
   Learning his Love, ...*

2. Whose memorial plaque bears the words 'Death is the enemy. Against you I will fling myself unvanquished and unyielding, O Death!'?

3. Mark Sharp's gravestone in the churchyard of St John sub Castro at Lewes is carved with the tools of his trade. How did he earn his living?

4. In which village church will you find a memorial to members of the local cricket team who were killed in the first world war, with the words 'They played the game'?

5. Where will you come across a plaque bearing the words 'They came to an enchanted place'?

6. Which downland memorial remembers men who 'passed through the fire'?

7. What's the unusual advice given at the end of Thomas Tipper's epitaph in St Michael's churchyard at Newhaven?

8. Where will you find a memorial to Finnish prisoners who died in Sussex during the Crimean War?

9. In which parish church is there a plaque to the great Archbishop of Canterbury Stephen Langton, one of the authors of Magna Carta?

10. What, according to his tombstone at Warnham, was Michael Turner doing when he died?

9. VILLAGES

Though Slindon is a little spot
Its fame has travelled far;
There's scarce another place, I wot,
Wherein such wonders are begot
As Slindon's wonders are.

Potatoes grow to monstrous size,
And marvels daily come
Beneath the gaze of Slindon's eyes
That cause all neighbours huge surprise,
And misbelief in some.

(W. Victor Cooke)

1. Which West Sussex village takes its name from a Norman baron called De Cahanges?

2. The wealthy racehorse owner Ambrose Gorham bequeathed his estate to Brighton Corporation in the 1930s, so ensuring that a Downland hamlet should remain unspoilt. Which one?

3. Several villages have the prefix 'Upper', but which two begin with 'Up'?

4. Which feature of Lurgashall has been moved to the Weald and Downland Open Air Museum at Singleton?

5. Which village can boast a public school, a reservoir and a showground?

6. How do you pronounce the village names Easebourne, Offham and Oving?

7. The people of Chailey 'beat the bounds' of their parish every year. How many miles must they walk?

8. A Meteor jet piloted by a local man crashed on an East Sussex village in January, 1956. Which one?

9. Only two Sussex villages have double-barrelled names (apart from Easts and Wests, Uppers, Lowers and the like). Which are they?

10. In which year were elected parish councils introduced, transferring power from the church and the lords of the manor to the ordinary people of the countryside?

10. WRITERS

'James regarded his fellow creatures with a face of distress and a remote effort at intercourse, like some victim of enchantment in the centre of an immense bladder. His life was unbelievably correct and his home at Rye one of the most perfect pieces of suitably furnished Georgian architecture imaginable.'

(H.G.Wells being less than kind about Henry James, who lived and worked at Lamb House in Rye

1. Which novelist lived at Uppark, where his mother was housekeeper?

2. Which writer journeyed through Sussex in the 1820s, collecting material for the book that was to become 'Rural Rides'?

3. In which village near Arundel is the fantasy writer Mervyn Peake buried?

4. Which 20th century playwright lived for some years at Hellingly Mill?

5. Which poet was baptised at Warnham church on September 7, 1792?

6. Stella Gibbons used Sussex as the setting for a comic novel whose heroine was alerted to 'something nasty in the woodshed'. What was its title?

7. Anthony Trollope wrote four novels while living in a West Sussex village towards the end of his life. Which one?

8. Which Elizabethan dramatist was born in Rye?

9. Rudyard Kipling's guest book at Bateman's has the letters 'FIP' against the names of some visitors. What do they signify?

10. The poet W.H. Davies, who was married at East Grinstead in February 1923, and who is best known for the lines 'What is this life if full of care/We have no time to stand and stare...' had a physical handicap. What was it?

11. THE YEAR IN QUESTION

A plaque in Jevington church seems uncertain about the year in which a former rector, Nathaniel Collier, went to meet his Maker: 'dyed Mar. ye first 169½'. The apparent confusion probably reflects religious politics, however. The Old Style calendar still in force in England began on March 25, whereas the New Style adopted by Roman Catholic countries since 1582 counted from January 1. Collier, who refused to take the oath of allegiance to the Protestant William and Mary in 1689, probably liked to believe that he passed away in 1692, whatever anyone else might think.

In which year:

1. Was the first turnpike trust formed in Sussex in order to improve the county's appalling roads?

2. Did the first regular mail coaches run from London to Brighton?

3. Did the last public execution take place at Horsham?

4. Did Glyndebourne opera house stage its first public performance?

5. Was the Royal Sussex Regiment formed?

6. Did Queen Victoria first visit Brighton?

7. Did the Black Death reach Sussex?

8. Was Chichester given its market cross?

9. Did the Swing Riots break out in Sussex?

10. Was the first cuckoo fair held at Heathfield?

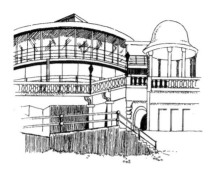

12. BRICKS AND MORTAR

In honour of Uppark, the beautiful seventeenth century house near South Harting which, though gutted by fire in August 1989, is now open to the public once again after a painstaking restoration by the National Trust.

1. Which renowned building did the architects Mendelsohn and Chermayeff design on the Sussex coast in the 1930s?

2. In good light you can see that the tower of St Mary's Church in Eastbourne's Old Town has a definite green tinge. Why?

3. Which Sussex landmark was used as a location for the TV adaptation of Fay Weldon's *Life & Loves of a She Devil?*

4. Which Sussex house, which sits on the edge of a famous garden, was built for John Baker Holroyd?

5. Dr Richard Russell popularised the sea-water cure at Brighton. Which hotel now stands at the spot where he built his house in the 1750s?

6. In which town is there a house shaped and coloured like a piece of cheese?

7. In Georgian times many buildings in Brighton and Lewes were faced with tiles, often to disguise their timber framing behind apparent brickwork. What name is given to them?

8. In which stately home will you find wood carvings by the great Grinling Gibbons?

9. Which Sussex house is the home of Viscount Hampden?

10. Which architect was responsible for the first buildings on the University of Sussex campus?

13. THIS SPORTING LIFE

'When batting...he sent his ball into the middle of the sheet of water, where it could be seen floating about, and so could not be called a lost ball. On that ball my father obtained twenty-four runs, before anybody waded into the water after it.'

(Edward Boys Ellman - 'Recollections of a Sussex Parson' - on a match at Seaford between 'public and private school men')

1. In which year was the first match played at the county cricket ground in Hove?

2. What did Captain Cuttle and Coronach achieve?

3. Which Peacehaven sportswoman has been world champion over and over again?

4. Which Sussex town hosts an international chess tournament every year?

5. With which sport has Bob Dugard been associated with for many years?

6. A familiar television sports presenter once sold insurance in Sussex. Who is he?

7. Which sport is played at Beach House Park, Worthing?

8. What's the name of the golf course near Uckfield which has staged the European Open championship?

9. Name the four Sussex race courses.

10. Which sport has its British Board of Control based at the Greyhound Hotel, Frimley Green?

14. MISCELLANEOUS

A wide-ranging round dedicated to the scholar-shepherd John Dudeney, born in Plumpton on April 21, 1782. He began tending sheep at the age of eight and for the next fifteen years bought and read as many books as money and time would allow. When he was twenty-three and self-educated in arithmetic, algebra, geometry, history and a great deal more, he left the hills to become a schoolmaster in Lewes.

1. Which were the two largest Sussex towns in 1750?

2. Which Sussex author's first book was called 'A Song for Every Season'?

3. Which two singers jointly bought Socknersh Manor, near Burwash, during the 1970s?

4. Which organisation founded by the science fiction writer L. Ron Hubard has its UK headquarters near East Grinstead?

5. Amberley 1377, Bodiam 1384, Herstmonceux 1440: what do the figures signify?

6. There are only two towns along the whole range of the South Downs. Which are they?

7. What's strange about the position of Camber Castle, built by Henry VIII to defend Rye Bay?

8. Who was the last 'gentleman' cricketer to captain Sussex?

9. Which prestigious Sussex building was designed by the architect Sir Michael Hopkins?

10. What sits at the centre of a Sussex pond pudding?

15. THE WAY WE WERE

The first of May is Garland Day,
So please remember the garland.
We don't come here but once a year,
So please remember the garland.

(Song traditionally sung by children parading
through the streets with flowers and a
collecting box)

1. Which kind of creature did Sussex country folk think would cure jaundice if you swallowed it live and rolled up in butter?

2. Complete the old saying:
   Sussex born and Sussex bred,
   Strong in the arm..........

3. What sort of a drink was 'flannel' in Old Sussex?

4. And what was a 'plum-heavy'?

5. What, to bring yourself luck, were you supposed to do if you found a pebble with a hole in it on a Sussex beach?

6. What, according to legend, will happen if you run seven times backwards around Chanctonbury Ring?

7. Which annual ceremony was known as 'Hollerin' Pot'?

8. What was a 'virgin's wreath'?

9. One of the rites of spring in Sussex was bat-and-trap. What was it?

10. Elderly women used to go from house to house on St Thomas's Day, December 21st, collecting ingredients for the Christmas feast. What name was given to this day of charity?

16. TOWNS

'The plan is clear and clean and rational - a thing of beauty having unity, proportion and clarity'

(the artist and typographer Eric Gill, eulogising Chichester)

1. In which town are the road names arranged in alphabetical order in each district, starting at the centre and working outwards?

2. When was 'Brighton', rather than 'Brighthelmstone', officially adopted as the name of the town?

3. In which town's high street will you find the Pelham Arms, the White Hart and the Rainbow Tavern?

4. Which town has Golden Square at its centre?

5. In which town does the high street run into Upper Lake?

6. Which town boasts both a port and an airport?

7. In which town is the raised pavement of the High Street architecturally listed?

8. Where in Sussex will you find an Avenue de Chartres?

9. And where can you walk along Turkeycock Lane?

10. Which town did Dr Leeson Prince promote at the end of the nineteenth century by praising its fresh air and healthy produce?

17. WILLDLIFE

*'And so the last stage of my journey to Kingley Vale
began on foot - which is a good way to face any
encounter, giving one time to prepare onself, the
physical exertion removing any feelings of dread
within the pit of the stomach. For a little way the
downs hid behind a woodland of tall old beech trees
and some oaks and yews. By the field gate was an ivy-
covered hawthorn bush, and out of this flew a small
black and white bird which sat above me on the beech
branches flicking its wings. It was the first pied
flycatcher that I had ever seen.'*

(Richard Williamson, 'The Great Yew Forest')

1. How many species of wild deer are there in Sussex?

2. To the nearest hundred, how many species of beetle have been recorded in the county?

3. Which two ancient Sussex deer parks still have herds of fallow deer in them?

4. Which of the following is *not* found in the wild in Sussex: edible frog, red-necked wallaby, mink, red squirrel, ring-necked parakeet?

5. Which tree did Kipling refer to as 'the Sussex weed'?

6. The Forestry Commission owns Friston Forest. Which is the principal tree grown there?

7. How many species of flea have been recorded in Sussex?

8. Which of these trees is *not* a native of Sussex: oak, Scots pine, sycamore?

9. Which bat, last seen at a roost in Sussex, became extinct in Britain during the 1990s?

10. Which downland flower is known as 'the pride of Sussex'?

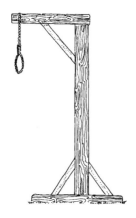

18. DEATH NOTICES

Scatter my ashes!
Hereby I make it a trust;
I in no grave be confined,
Mingle my dust with the dust,
Give me in fee to the wind!
Scatter my ashes!

(John Galsworthy, whose ashes were duly
scattered on Bury Hill on March 28, 1933)

1. When did the last serious smallpox outbreak occur in Brighton, claiming ten lives?

2. Ten people were killed and 26 injured in a bush crash on a steep Sussex hill on July 12, 1906. Which one?

3. Twenty-three people were killed and nearly two hundred injured in a rail crash near Brighton on August 25, 1861. Where exactly?

4. A gravestone at Kirdford commemorates five lads who died together. What was the cause of death?

5. What morbid nickname was given to Brighton, that celebrated 'Queen of Watering Places', after the notorious 'trunk murders' of 1934?

6. For what crime was Edmund Bushby of East Preston hanged on New Year's Day, 1831?

7. A stone commemorates the hanging of several murderous smugglers. In which Sussex town?

8. What the Brightonian James 'Jemmy' Botting did for a living gave him ghastly visions in his later years. What was his job?

9. Two gravestones in the churchyard at Walberton, near Bognor Regis, record accidental deaths. Charles Cook was hit by a falling tree, but how did eight-year-old Ann Rusbridger meet her end?

10. For what was John Story, the Roman Catholic MP for East Grinstead, hung, drawn and quartered at Tyburn in 1571?

19. PARKS AND GARDENS

'It is later than you think.'

(Sundial motto in the garden of Rudyard
Kipling's house, Bateman's at Burwash)

1. The tallest tree in Sussex is a grand fir in Eridge Park which stands above 150ft. Which famous politican planted it?

2. What's unusual about the garden run by Worthing borough council at Highdown?

3. What have the gardens at Petworth House, Sheffield Park and Ashburnham, near Battle, in common?

4. Which Sussex garden is leased to the Royal Botanic Gardens at Kew?

5. Which Sussex-based writer wrote 'The Glory of the Garden'?

6. Which family created the notable High Weald gardens at Leonardslee, High Beeches and Wakehurst Place?

7. Which famous garden was bought by Ludwig Messel in 1908?

8. Which Sussex garden is owned by the Stephenson Clarke family?

9. The tree with the biggest girth in East Sussex is growing on the Beauport Park estate and measures 33ft. What kind of tree is it?

10. In which West Sussex village will you find Red Oaks, the home for retired gardeners?

20. SUSSEX BOOK OF RECORDS

Dedicated to Boxgrove Man, otherwise known as Roger, who lived here 500,000 years ago - the earliest of our ancestors yet to be discovered in Europe.
A solitary fragment of one of his shin bones was unveiled to the world in 1994.

1. The world's deepest hand-dug well lies below the former Fitzherbert School in Woodingdean, Brighton. How deep is it?

2. What's probably the world's oldest cricket ball has been discovered inside the wall of a Lewes house. From which year, approximately, does it date?

3. The world's first permanent lifeboat museum opened in Sussex in 1937. In which seaside town?

4. The world's oldest photography business operates in Lewes. Which is it?

5. Now more than 130 years old, the open-air swimming pool in Lewes is claimed to be the oldest in the country. What is its name?

Where will you find:

6. The world's oldest licensed commercial airfield?

7. The longest Roman mosaic in Britain?

8. The largest Roman palace in northern Europe?

9. Britain's highest chalk cliffs?

10. What's claimed to be the smallest barber's shop in the world?

21. DIALECT

'Yer teeth be lik a flock of ship just shared, dat come up from de ship-wash.'

(from a Sussex dialect version of The Song of Solomon by the historian Mark Antony Lower)

1. What did it mean, in Old Sussex, to 'beat the devil about the gooseberry bush'?

2. An important man at a wedding was the 'old-father'. What was his role?

3. Why might someone's house be called 'a mock-beggar-hall'?

4. What, to a pig farmer, was a 'dawlin' (or 'darling')?

5. You might need a jossing-block in order to joss-up. What would you be doing?

6. A village a few miles from Lewes was once known as 'Charnton' by Sussex dialect speakers. We follow the spelling today. Which village is it?

7. Who were your 'clawney'?

8. It wasn't complimentary to be called a 'blobtit'. What did it mean?

9. What was a 'grummut'?

10. And what did it mean to be 'concerned in liquor'?

22. COME RAIN, COME SHINE

When Foxes-brewings go to Cocking
Foxes-brewings come back dropping.

(ancient weather lore, forecasting rain if the
downland mists known as 'foxes-brewings'
should veer westwards towards Cocking)

1. The highest temperature ever recorded in Sussex was at Plumpton on July 1, 1976. How hot was it?

2. And what was the *lowest* temperature, recorded at Bodiam in January, 1940?

3. On which date did the so-called 'hurricane' of 1987 wreak havoc in Sussex?

4. The highest wind speed in Sussex was recorded at Shoreham during the hurricane. What was it?

5. The hurricane was the worst storm of its kind since a well-documented tornado devastated the county centuries before. In which year?

6. What, weather-wise, did these years have in common for Sussex: 1890, 1927, 1947, 1967, 1987?

7. Eastbourne is Britain's sunniest seaside resort. How many hours of sunshine does it average a day during high summer?

8. The wettest day ever recorded in Sussex was October 10, 1980, when the wettest *place* was Durrington. How many inches of rain fell there?

9. Which was the warmest month in Sussex since the war?

10. And the coldest?

23. RELIGIOUS TYPES

'I went back to Shoreham. Mr P., though in his eighty-fifth year, is still able to go through the whole Sunday service. How merciful is God to the poor people of Shoreham! And many of them are not insensible of it.'

(John Wesley's Journal, January 1778)

1. What, during the 16th century, did these families have in common: the Gages at Firle, the Carylls at West Grinstead, the Palmers at Parham and the Howards at Arundel?

2. The Quaker founder of an American state lived in Warminghurst. Who was he?

3. Which great Baptist preacher lived for many years at Bexhill?

4. Whose prayer ends: 'May I know Thee more clearly/Love Thee more dearly/ And follow Thee more nearly'?

5. Puritans often gave their children outlandish names such as Fearnot and Bethankfull. What did the Richardsons of Waldron call their son to discourage him from vice?

6. Accepted Frewen, son of a Puritan rector, became Archbishop of York in 1660. Where in Sussex did the Frewen family live?

7. Which great churchman, who later converted to Rome, began his career as an Anglican and was curate in charge at the tiny apsidal church of Upwaltham?

8. In the church at Westham, near Pevensey, is a small piece of stone brought here in 1860 by the vicar, Howard Hopley, after he had visited an important archaeological site in the Holy Land. What did the fragment come from?

9. Above which town is there a memorial to seventeen Protestants who were burned to death during the Marian persecutions?

10. Which fitting text can be seen on the tombstone of Samuel Sparrow, the first organist of St Wilfrid's Church in Haywards Heath?

24. INDUSTRIAL HISTORY

A round in honour of Thomas Smith of Herstmonceux, inventor of the Sussex trug, whose family is still manufacturing this indispensable gardening basket several generations later.

1. Where will you find the last conical brick-built kiln in Sussex?

2. What name was given to the pottery produced in Sussex from the late eighteenth century to the early twentieth century?

3. The British Engineerium in Hove is a museum celebrating engineering ingenuity. What was the building's original function?

4. A former chalk pit in West Sussex is the home of a major industrial history museum. Where is it?

5. What did the Romans produce in a bloomery?

6. In which town will you find the nine-arched Imberhorne railway viaduct?

7. A strange domed building squats near the library in London Road, Bognor Regis. What is it?

8. A water-pumping station installed in 1782 to supply water to Petworth $1^1/_2$ miles away can still be seen beside the River Rother. Where?

9. In 1903 Rudyard Kipling removed the waterwheel from the mill at Bateman's and installed a water turbine. For what purpose?

10. What have Clayton, Cross-in-Hand, High Salvington and Nutley in common?

25. RIVERS

'Hee is likewise against the second of August yearly being the swann-hooking or swan-hopping day to summon owners of swanns that have swan markes on the stream to see their young signetts marked, and taken up if they desire it, paying for marking every signett 4d, taking any up vid.'

(Swan-upping duties of the water bailiff on the River Arun)

1. Groombridge is split between Sussex and Kent. Which river forms the boundary?

2. Which river was once known as Bramber Water?

3. Where does the Wallers Haven river meet the sea?

4. By which river does Alfriston stand?

5. What do the Winterbourne stream in Lewes and the Lavant in Chichester have in common?

6. Which name is common to two rivers, one in East Sussex, the other in West Sussex?

7. The writer E.F. Benson thinly disguised his home town of Rye in the Mapp & Lucia books under a name derived from a local river. Which one?

8. Our largest Sussex river rises in St Leonard's Forest. Which is it?

9. Which Sussex river was known as Midewinde in medieval times?

10. Three Bridges, Crawley, derives its name from its river crossings. But over which river?

26. MISCELLANEOUS

Having dedicated the previous miscellany round to the scholar-shepherd John Dudeney, we this time honour his namesake Henry Dudeney, a notable all-rounder known as 'the puzzle king'. Born at Mayfield on April 10, 1857, he was an excellent organist and pianist, a skilful player of games as varied as chess, billiards and croquet, and the greatest mathematical puzzler of the age. He wrote three books on the subject and is said to have been the first mathematician to deal with the digital roots of numbers.

1. What have Waterloo, Commercial Square and Cliffe in common?

2. What will you find on the Downs at Lullington Heath, Kingston and Newtimber Hill?

3. In 1519 Sir Henry Guldeford of East Guldeford fought for Spain against the Moors, and was granted a fitting 'augmentation of honour' on his family's coat of arms. Which device was added to it?

4. The original Gipsy Lee was consulted by many famous people, among them Mr Gladstone. Where did she keep her caravan?

5. Which is the southernmost railway station north of Brighton at which you can board trains bound for either Brighton or Hastings?

6. Which traditional rural implement had a handle made of ash or hazel and a metal end which was said to be best when fashioned from an old gun barrel?

7. How did Decimus Burton, the man who completed the building of St Leonards, get his first name?

8. The old Nineveh Shipyard building became a sawmill and produced tent pegs for the Army during the Boer War. Where is it?

9. Which famous actor has written about his childhood in Sussex, when he lived at the Old Rectory in Lullington?

10. Which perfectly-formed Ardingly schoolboy went on to edit *Private Eye* magazine?

27. SCHOOLS

'This day I entertained my scholars with the sight of a show which was at Jones's; the man performed in my schoolroom. I think it a very good performance of the kind. He performed several very curious balances, ate fire and red hot tobacco-pipes, brimstone etc. I gave him 12d.'

(from Thomas Turner's diary)

1. What's the other name by which Christ's Hospital school, near Horsham, is known?

2. Of which West Sussex school does the 16th century Brotherhood Hall form a part?

3. It lies between Blackwater Road and Carlisle Road.

4. What was originally known as 'The Guild of Brave Poor Things'?

5. In which Mid Sussex village will you find Downlands School?

6. 'The fear of the Lord is the beginning of wisdom' is a text carved round the door of a former village schoolhouse. In which West Sussex village?

7. Which twentieth century prime minister was stabbed in the chest while a pupil at Lansworth House School, Hove, in 1884?

8. In which school's grounds is there a Queen Anne chess garden, the board laid out in black and white chippings and the pieces fashioned from trained yew trees?

9. In which year was Brighton College founded?

10. What do the initials BHASVIC stand for?

28. FOLLIES

A round inevitably dedicated to John 'Mad Jack' Fuller, the most dedicated of Sussex folly-builders, whose peculiar pyramidal mausoleum is pictured on the cover of the first book in this series.

1. Thomas Attree had a five-storey tower built close to Queen's Park in Brighton in the 1830s, apparently intending it to be an observatory. What is it commonly known as today?

2. The Countess of Newburgh ordered the building of a flint folly on her estate at Slindon, and the remains still stand two hundred years later. What is its name?

3. Edward James gave the folly treatment to two beech trees on his West Dean estate, near Chichester. What's strange about them?

4. Look south while driving along the A27 and you'll see a circular gamekeeper's tower with turrets. Where?

5. The Prince Regent used to carouse in the Vandalian Tower, a hilltop folly in the grounds of a grand house. Which one?

6. There's a folly inside the grounds of Petworth House, too. What is it known as?

7. The Toat Monument near Pulborough remembers Samuel Drinkald, who was killed at the spot. How?

8. On whose land will you see the Saxonbury Tower, erected in 1828 with the letters *HA* appearing over the door under a coronet?

9. The Hiorne Tower at Arundel was designed by Francis Hiorne for the eleventh Duke of Norfolk. But for what purpose?

10. Where can you see a toll house in the form of a tiny castle?

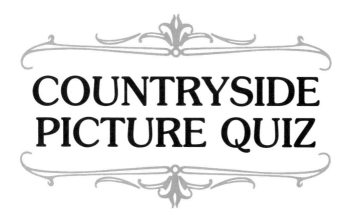

COUNTRYSIDE PICTURE QUIZ

1. The Old Cottage sports elaborate carvings of animals, angels and a host of grotesque figures. In which village east of Lewes will you find it?

2. The remnant of a moated manor house. Near which village?

3. *For the field is full of shades*
   as I near the shadowy coast,
   And a ghostly batsman plays
   to the bowling of a ghost.

In which West Sussex churchyard was Alban Barchard laid to rest?

4. This former inn sign can now be seen *inside* The Swan. Where?

5. This parish pump, installed in 1883, sits by a large village green in East Sussex. Where?

6. A thatched well and a fine 13th century flint church. Where in remote West Sussex will you find them?

7. Commandment tables painted on plaster above the chancel arch of a 12th century church set in parkland in the far east of the county. In which village?

8.

MY FRIENDS SO
DEAR AS YOU PASS
BY SOE AS YOU ARE
SOE ONCE WAS I
AND AS I AM
SOE SHALL YOU BE
REMEMBER
DEATH AND
THINK ON ME

This gravestone with its sombre message stands by the path which leads to an ancient West Sussex church. Which one?

9. 'The smallest house in Sussex' has one room upstairs and one down, yet was once home to a family of five. Where is it?

10. This fine old granary on staddle stones can be seen in the grounds of a once-great house which now lies in ruins. It's in a rural setting, although on the edge of an historic West Sussex town. Where is it?

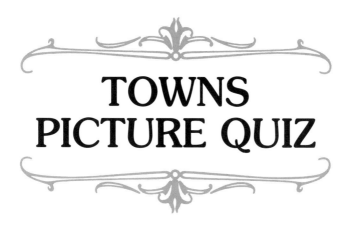

TOWNS
PICTURE QUIZ

1. Almshouses for the poor. In which West Sussex town?

2. Those figures above the clock ring the quarter-hours. Where?

3. An ancient building in a coastal town. Which one?

4. Horsham, of course. But where will you find it?

5. Mathematical tiles clad this house. Where are we?

6. Pulpitt Gate is a modern house which incorporates a number of
   unusual features, including a huge stone window, a Jacobean
   staircase and a well in the dining room. Where is it?

7. The elegance of an imported bandstand in a functional shopping square. Where?

8. The ironmongers shop, with the anvil perched on its gable, has been here for more than a hundred years. Where are we?

9. The ancient church stands above and to one side of the old town, formerly enclosed by North Street, East Street, West Street and the sea. What's the name of the church?

10. What's the name of the covered shopping centre beyond the trees?

ANSWERS

1. SUSSEX BY THE SEA

1. The third was for sea water, raised by a pump installed in Grand Avenue in 1872.
2. Because they are converted railway carriages, partly disguised by modern pebble-dashing and the like. Between the two world wars there were several shanty towns along the Sussex coast.
3. The promontory was demolished in 1834 so that the seafront could be extended westwards to St Leonards.
4. Peacehaven.
5. Worthing.
6. It's a designated area for naturists. I well remember first visiting it, unawares, with binoculars around my neck for bird-watching.
7. Shoreham Beach.
8. Newhaven.
9. It's inland!
10. The West Pier at Brighton.

2. SOMETHING IN COMMON

1. Village ponds.
2. They were all built for Sussex ironmasters.
3. Youth hostels.
4. They're all former workhouses.
5. Moats.
6. Windmills.
7. Reservoirs.
8. Police stations.
9. Both regularly took their holidays at Eastbourne.
10. Tithe barns, or their remains.

3. MISCELLANEOUS

1. Water. Until its electrification in 1974 it was one of the country's last water-balance cliff railways, with tanks holding 600 gallons.
2. Medieval rabbit warrens.
3. At Haywards Heath. (The Roundheads won it).
4. Glass-making.
5. The White House in Washington.
6. He planted the Grand Hotel bomb in 1984.
7. Sweet chestnut and willow.
8. Rodin's 'The Kiss', which he'd commissioned himself and which can now be seen in the Tate Gallery. The local council feared that it might dangerously inflame the passions of injured soldiers home from the trenches of the first world war.
9. Hove Museum & Art Gallery.
10. Pumice.

4. A WOMAN'S WORLD

1. A school for lady gardeners.
2. Selina Shirley, Countess of Huntingdon.
3. Tilly Losch.
4. A car park for women only.
5. Ladies Mile Road.
6. Charlotte Bronte.
7. At Lewes.
8. Gracie Fields, in Peacehaven.
9. Morris dancing.
10. The institution which later became Chailey Heritage.

5. CHURCHES

1. At Ifield, now part of Crawley.
2. You pass through a farmyard to reach it.
3. A carpet of flowers.
4. The Seven Deadly Sins.
5. A barrel organ.
6. St John the Baptist in Bristol Road, Brighton.
7. The original windows were blown out by a bomb during the second world war.
8. The one at Rye: 'For our time is a very shadow that passeth away.'
9. Sussex caps.
10. A reproduction of Michelangelo's masterpiece on the ceiling of the Vatican's Sistine Chapel. It took him five years.

6. ON THE ROAD

1. At Lewes.
2. Cowfold.
3. The A24 is the only one running north-south rather than east-west.
4. At Beddingham.
5. Bury
6. Mileposts dating from the turnpikes of the eighteenth century.
7. The B2118.
8. Into it.
9. The A259 and the A27.
10. Midhurst.

7. DRINK AND BE MERRY

1. Freddy Mercury, the former lead singer of the rock group Queen. It was later replaced by a more traditional playing card design.

2. The Bull.

3. Rose Cottage.

4. A tourist information centre.

5. The Gardeners Arms.

6. The Lamb.

7. Animal Farm.

8. In Lindfield.

9. The Old Ship.

10. The Royal Oak.

8. GONE BUT NOT FORGOTTEN

1. *Consumption his Fate.*

2. Virginia Woolf's, at Rodmell.

3. As a carpenter.

4. Ringmer.

5. On Ashdown Forest. It commemorates A.A.Milne, creator of the Winnie-the-Pooh stories, and his illustrator, E.H. Shepard.

6. The Chattri, north of Patcham. The bodies of Sikh and Hindu soldiers who died in hospital at the Royal Pavilion during the first world war had previously been burned on a ghat at the same spot.

7. 'Be better, wiser; laugh more if you can.'

8. In the churchyard of St John sub Castro, Lewes. Some 350 of the, captured at the Battle of Bomarsund in 1854, were held at Lewes Naval Prison.

9. Slindon.

10. Playing the violin: *'And when at last his age had passed/One hundred less eleven/With faithful cling to fiddle string/He sang himself to heaven.'*

9. VILLAGES

1. Horsted Keynes.
2. Telscombe.
3. Up Marden and Upwaltham, both in West Sussex.
4. Its watermill.
5. Ardingly.
6. Ezbourne, Oaf'm, Ooving.
7. 24 miles
8. Wadhurst.
9. Horsted Keynes and Tarring Neville.
10. 1894. The story has been told in two centenary books, Valerie Porter's 'The Village Parliaments' for West Sussex, and my own 'Tales of the Parish Pump' for East Sussex.

10. WRITERS

1. H.G.Wells.
2. William Cobbett.
3. Burpham.
4. John Osborne, author of 'Look Back in Anger' and 'The Entertainer'.
5. Shelley.
6. Cold Comfort Farm.
7. South Harting.
8. John Fletcher.
9. Fell in pond.
10. He had only one leg.

11. THE YEAR IN QUESTION

1. 1749
2. 1810.
3. 1844. John Lawrence was hanged for killing Brighton's police superintendent, Henry Solomon, with a poker.
4. 1934.
5. 1701.
6. 1837.
7. 1349.
8. 1501.
9. 1830.
10. 1315.

12. BRICKS AND MORTAR

1. The De La Warr Pavilion at Bexhill.
2. Because it's made of the local greensand.
3. Belle Tout lighthouse, on the cliffs west of Eastbourne.
4. Sheffield Park.
5. The Royal Albion.
6. Hastings, in All Saints Street.
7. Mathematical tiles.
8. Petworth House.
9. Glynde Place.
10. Sir Basil Spence.

13. THIS SPORTING LIFE

1. 1872.
2. They were Sussex-bred racehorses which won the Derby.
3. Allison Fisher.
4. Hastings.
5. Speedway.
6. Desmond Lynam. He began his broadcasting career with the former BBC Radio Brighton.
7. Bowls. The national championships are held here.
8. The East Sussex National.
9. Brighton, Fontwell, Goodwood and Plumpton.
10. Marbles. The world championships are held at Frimley Green every Good Friday.

14. MISCELLANEOUS

1. Lewes and Chichester.
2. Bob Copper.
3. Tom Jones and Engelbert Humperdinck.
4. The Church of Scientology.
5. The dates when the castles were fortified.
6. Arundel and Lewes.
7. It's now a mile inland, thanks to the shingle which has been desposited over the centuries.
8. Ted Dexter.
9. The new Glyndebourne.
10. The answer is a lemon!

15. THE WAY WE WERE

1. A spider.
2. *And weak in the head!*
3. Hot spiced beer.
4. A small round cake made of pie-crust, and having raisins or currants in it.
5. Spit through the hole and throw the pebble over your left shoulder.
6. The Devil will appear.
7. The gathering of farm workers, when they had finished bringing the harvest home, to chant the song: 'We've ploughed, we've sowed, we've reaped, we've mowed,/We've carried the last load, and ne'er overthrowed,/Hip, hip, hurrah!'
8. A garland of white flowers hung in a church after the funeral of a young girl or, in some places, a widow who had had only one husband. The custom seems to have persisted at Alfriston longer than in other parts of Sussex.
9. A game involving batsmen and fielders. The ball was projected from the trap, a piece of wood shaped like a carpenter's plane.
10. Gooding Day. The women were known as Gooders.

16. TOWNS

1. Crawley New Town. The man responsible, John Goepel, also left a cryptogram of his surname in the Tilgate area, where streets are named after Cathedrals: Gloucester, Oxford, Exeter, Peterborough, Ely and Lincoln.
2. As recently as 1810.
3. Lewes.
4. Petworth.
5. Battle. Upper Lake is the name of the street which passes the parish church.
6. Shoreham.
7. Hastings, in the Old Town.
8. In Chichester.
9. In Rye.
10. Crowborough.

17. WILDLIFE

1. Four: fallow, roe, muntjac and sika.
2. 2,800.
3. Petworth and Parham.
4. The red squirrel.
5. The oak.
6. Beech.
7. 36.
8. Sycamore.
9. The mouse-eared bat.
10. The round-headed rampion.

18. DEATH NOTICES

1. In 1950. An RAF officer introduced the disease to the town on his return from India.
2. Handcross Hill.
3. In the Clayton Tunnel.
4. They 'placed green wood ashes in their bedroom' - and were presumably asphyxiated.
5. 'The Queen of Slaughtering Places'.
6. Setting fire to one of his employer's haystacks during the so-called Swing Riots.
7. Chichester. The stone stands in Broyle Road.
8. He was the public executioner.
9. She was struck by a barrel which fell from a runaway cart.
10. Treason - 'inciting the Duke of Alba to invade England.'

19. PARKS AND GARDENS

1. Benjamin Disraeli.
2. It's a chalk garden.
3. All were designed, in part, by Capability Brown.
4. Wakehurst Place.
5. Rudyard Kipling.
6. The Loders.
7. Nymans.
8. Borde Hill.
9. A Monterrey Cypress.
10. Henfield.

20. SUSSEX BOOK OF RECORDS

1. 1,285ft. It took paupers from the old Brighton Workhouse in Dyke Road four years to dig, finishing their toil in 1862.
2. 1770.
3. Eastbourne. (And it's still open).
4. Edward Reeves.
5. The Pells Pool.
6. At Shoreham.
7. At Bignor Roman villa.
8. At Fishbourne, near Chichester.
9. At Beachy Head: 534ft.
10. On the Palace Pier at Brighton.

21. DIALECT

1. To tell a long and pointless story.
2. He was the man (often the sweetheart of the bridesmaid) who gave away the bride at her wedding.
3. The term referred to a house which was imposing from the outside but threadbare within.
4. The smallest pig in a litter.
5. Riding a horse. To joss-up was to mount it and the jossing-block was the mounting-block.
6. Chalvington. (And nearby Selmeston was 'Simpson').
7. Your ancestors and family relations.
8. That you were a tell-tale.
9. An awkward boy.
10. Drunk!

22. COME RAIN, COME SHINE

1. 35.6 Centigrade (about 96 F)
2. 21.2 Centigrade (about - 6 F)
3. October 16, 1987.
4. 115 miles per hour.
5. 1729. Houses and barns were flattened, and thousands of trees were uprooted, including 1400 on the Battle Abbey estate alone.
6. Heavy snowfalls.
7. Seven.
8. 5.25 inches.
9. July, 1983.
10. January, 1963.

23. RELIGIOUS TYPES

1. They were all staunch Roman Catholics.
2. William Penn, founder of Pennsylvania.
3. Charles Haddon Spurgeon.
4. St Richard of Chichester's.
5. Fly-Fornication.
6. In Northiam.
7. Cardinal Manning.
8. King Solomon's temple in Jerusalem.
9. Lewes.
10. 'Peace, perfect peace.'

24. INDUSTRIAL HISTORY

1. At Piddinghoe.
2. Brownware.
3. It was the Goldstone pumping station, built in 1866 to raise water from deep in the chalk to supply the rapidly-growing communities of Brighton and Hove. One of the original beam engines is still in place, and working.
4. Next to Amberley railway station.
5. Iron.
6. East Grinstead.
7. An ice house. It was built for the Hotham Estate around 1797.
8. At Coultershaw Bridge.
9. To drive a generator which supplied light to the house.
10. Post windmills.

25. RIVERS

1. The Medway.
2. The Adur.
3. At Norman's Bay, near Pevensey.
4. The Cuckmere.
5. They flow for only part of the year.
6. Rother.
7. The Tillingham. Benson called Rye 'Tilling'.
8. The Arun.
9. The Ouse.
10. The Mole.

26. MISCELLANEOUS

1. They're three of the five Lewes bonfire societies.
2. Dewponds.
3. A pomegranate.
4. At Devil's Dyke.
5. Wivelsfield Green.
6. A shepherd's crook.
7. He was the tenth child of the town's founder, James Burton.
8. At Arundel.
9. Dirk Bogarde.
10. Ian Hislop. (The 'perfectly-formed' tag refers to his diminutive size).

27. SCHOOLS

1. The Bluecoat School. It was founded at Chichester in 1712, with money left in the will of Oliver Whitby. The pupils were transferred to Christ's Hospital in 1951.
2. Steyning Grammar School.
3. Eastbourne College.
4. Chailey Heritage.
5. Hassocks.
6. Albourne.
7. Sir Winston Churchill, attacked by a boy whose ear he had pulled. Had the knife not penetrated his skin by only a quarter of an inch modern history might now read rather differently.
8. Brickwall at Northiam.
9. 1847.
10. Brighton Hove and Sussex Sixth Form College.

28. FOLLIES

1. The Pepper Pot.
2. The Nore Folly.
3. The trunks, complete with bracket fungus, have been preserved for all time in resin.
4. At Firle.
5. Uppark.
6. The Upperton Monument - though it's not a monument at all, but rather a lived-in folly designed to be a focus for the view north-west from Petworth House.
7. By falling from his horse.
8. The Marquis of Abergavenny's.
9. As an example of his work, so that he might win the contract for rebuilding the castle. Hiorne, however, died two years later at the age of 45.
10. Alongside the A280 between Clapham and Findon. It was built in 1820 as the Long Furlong toll house.

COUNTRYSIDE PICTURE QUIZ

1. At Ripe.
2. Laughton. The tower is all that remains of the original home of the powerful Pelham family.
3. Boxgrove. The churchyard also contains a gravestone commemorating Pilot Officer Bill Fiske, killed in action while stationed at Tangmere in 1940 and the first American serviceman to die in the second world war.
4. At Lower Fittleworth, near Pulborough.
5. In Ringmer.
6. East Marden.
7. Peasmarsh.
8. Worth.
9. At Northiam.
10. By the Cowdray Ruins, Easebourne, near Midhurst.

TOWNS PICTURE QUIZ

1. East Grinstead. This is Sackville College.
2. At Rye. They're known as the Quarterboys.
3. Shoreham. The building is The Marlipins.
4. In Pump Alley.
5. In Lewes - more precisely in School Hill, as the section of High Street below the war memorial is known. (The author craves forgiveness for self-indulgence: he once lived in this house).
6. In Hastings, near the foot of All Saints Street.
7. Crawley.
8. In Arundel.
9. St Nicholas, Brighton.
10. The Arndale Centre.

FRONT COVER PHOTOGRAPH: Chilgrove, near Chichester. The artist found a horse too challenging, so the owner suggested she paint something she was good at.

BACK COVER: The Pelham buckle, insignia of the powerful family which once lived at Laughton Place.